Somewhere Close to Dammaiguda Diaries

AMRITASH PRADHAN

BLUEROSE PUBLISHERS
India | U.K.

Copyright © Amritash Pradhan 2025

All rights reserved by author. No part of this publication may be reproduced, stored in a retrieval system or transmitted in any form or by any means, electronic, mechanical, photocopying, recording or otherwise, without the prior permission of the author. Although every precaution has been taken to verify the accuracy of the information contained herein, the publisher assumes no responsibility for any errors or omissions. No liability is assumed for damages that may result from the use of information contained within.

BlueRose Publishers takes no responsibility for any damages, losses, or liabilities that may arise from the use or misuse of the information, products, or services provided in this publication.

For permissions requests or inquiries regarding this publication, please contact:

BLUEROSE PUBLISHERS
www.BlueRoseONE.com
info@bluerosepublishers.com
+91 8882 898 898
+4407342408967

ISBN: 978-93-7018-498-5

Cover Design: Aman Sharma
Cover Illustrator: Amritash Pradhan

Typesetting: Pooja Sharma

First Edition: March 2025

To God, who wraps me in grace; to my family, my greatest support; to my teachers, my mentors in knowledge; to my friends, my adventure buddies—my first published book is for you!

Contents

Chapter 1: Nagesh: The First Friend 1

Chapter 2: The Cheek-Pulling Frenzy 4

Chapter 3: The Elections- Posters, Votes, and Dreams............ 7

Chapter 4: The Poster Incident.. 10

Chapter 5: Peacing It Out.. 12

Chapter 6: M.A.N... 15

Chapter 7: Blank Books- A Day at the Museum........................ 17

Chapter 8: Expressions 2022 19

Chapter 9: Seven Members.. 21

Chapter 10: M.A.N.'s Peak Time... 23

Chapter 11: Mumbai: A Walk Down Memory Lane 26

Chapter 12: Homecoming.. 31

Chapter 13: Presidential Perks and Pain 33

Chapter 14: Operation Spy 35

Chapter 15: The Fabric Drill 37

Chapter 16: A Splashy Day 40

Chapter 17: The Last Days of Grade 4 42

Acknowledgements 44

Chapter 1:

Nagesh: The First Friend

It was my first day at school. My parents dropped me off at the assembly. I wasn't in proper school uniform since I was new to this school. We had just moved from Mumbai, where I used to study at BHI School, Andheri. But as my mother ("Mamaa" to me) had recently gotten a job in Hyderabad, we had to shift. My new school was part of the same BHI chain of schools and followed the same curriculum and pedagogy as my old school. So, Mamaa decided to enroll me here to spare me from too many big changes.

By the time I was eight, I was already on my sixth school tour—starting in India, then moving to Djibouti, and back to India again! Mamaa always carefully chose schools where learning felt more like play and less like a test.

As I walked into the assembly ground, there was only one problem: I didn't know which section I was in. I knew I was in Grade 4, but what was my section? I ended up asking a Physical Education (PE) teacher, "Sir, which section do I have to go to?"

"Which grade?" the PE teacher asked.

"4th. 4th grade," I replied.

"Oh!" he said, "Go to the 4C line."

I went to look for 4C and fortunately found it.

After the assembly, I went to my new classroom. A few moments later, the class teacher arrived. She was thin, wore spectacles, and had an ID card from which I learned her name was Miss Shloka. She would be our Science and Technology teacher and **she** told me to sit next to a girl.

When I sat down, I spread my arms around the table, and the girl next to me shouted, "Eh, don't spread your arms around my table!!"

Umm…what? I thought. First of all, this is OUR table, not YOUR table. I also thought she could use a little lesson in manners.

Just as I was thinking this, Shloka Ma'am told me to move and sit on the third bench with a boy named Nagesh. He was mildly heavy-set with a darkish skin tone like mine. His hair was messy, and he wore a pink face mask. I sat on the empty seat next to him.

"We have two new students in our class!" announced Miss Shloka. "Their names are Pooja and Ametash."

"Amritash," I corrected her.

"Yes, Abhinash," she said, still getting it wrong. But I'm used to it by now. I think I've got the world's hardest name! I've asked my parents many times to change it to something simpler, but they always say it involves too much paperwork and requires permission from the government, blah, blah, blah… It's a tough life for a kid these days!

After breakfast, I went to guitar class with Nagesh. Our guitar teacher, Julius, wore a checkered T-shirt and blue jeans. He was also quite chubby. Not surprisingly, Nagesh gestured for me to sit next to him. I pretended not to see him and took a seat at the back. We learned the parts of a guitar (the head, neck, knee, body, and mouth) and then went back to class.

For the first time ever, after we got back to class, Nagesh removed his mask, and I could see his face. Nagesh wore his mask way too much, and as you know, too much of anything is bad, and Nagesh was a perfect example of that.

After the music class and a few others, it was lunchtime. By then, Nagesh and I had become good friends, and I seemed to be the smartest kid in class, which was nice. Just before lunch, Nagesh turned towards me and said in the most casual voice I'd ever heard…

"We make a good team, don't we?"

"Y-Yeah, I…I think so," I stammered.

"Don't you want to be friends?"

"Yeah."

I wanted my voice to sound as casual as Nagesh's, but it kept getting squeaky.

Nagesh extended his hand for me to shake, and I did. Nagesh and I were F.R.I.E.N.D.S. now.

Chapter 2:

The Cheek-Pulling Frenzy

Nagesh was my first friend in my new school, but to be honest, he was annoying.

First, he's a bit too much of a goody-two-shoes. Like, if you have a friend who's too good, then you can't play at all. Plus, this one time, I was running in the corridor, and for some reason, everybody started complaining to Nagesh. He came to me and said, "Did you run in the corridor?" in this fatherly sort of way, which, well, embarrassed me a lot.

Second, he always acts like a cartoon character. Like, if you even pretend to hit him, he overreacts (oooooowwwww!), ("You know what, I'm gonna tell Ma'am!") or, ("How dare I? How dare you!").

So, these are the reasons why Nagesh is not my best friend in the world. We don't like each other much, but we just peace it out.

But I also think my biggest weakness is Nagesh because if we became enemies, I'd have no one to support me. Nagesh has a few friends besides me, so being friends with him has become a necessity, even if I don't really like him.

Thinking about all this, I realized I really need friends. So, I started a sort of campaign: "Find someone and randomly pull their cheeks." The first victim of my campaign was Hardik Sastri... okay, that's the name other kids tease him with. I don't get how being named after a famous person is an insult, but yeah, his actual name is Hardik Sastri. He's tall, with chocolate brown skin, short black hair, and he's totally not my friend.

Between all this, Nagesh and I got into a big fight, which ended with me switching places with Peter (the tallest boy in class). Now my new partner is Vishnudas. He's as tall as me, fair, and wears thick blue plastic glasses.

There was one thing that told me we could be friends. One time I was humming the tune of "House of Memories" (by Panic! at the Disco), and I passed a table of five boys: Abdul (a pale, black-haired boy), Manian (the most popular boy in our class), Rajeev (a chubby, pale, and tall boy), and Vishnudas.

As I passed them, they started singing along, which felt like approval and potential friendship. I was going to make it official, and I did. But remember, the cheek-pulling campaign worked too.

In PE period, which is every Wednesday, I pulled the cheek of Shiv, a tall, weird, messy-haired boy, and he pulled my cheek back.

We had a whole war of cheek-pulling, which ended with Shiv and me becoming friends. And that's where the campaign shows its effect, see: everybody has a friend or best friend. So once you've made friends with even one person, their friends become your friends, and then their friend's friends become your friends, and so on.

This chain reaction certainly worked for me because when Shiv and I were waiting for our bus (Shiv and I travel on the same school bus), Shiv called Madhusmita—a slim, black girl—and told her to pull my cheeks. She did, and this was Cheek War II. When our bus came, Madhusmita sat beside me. When I thought we were friends, we both found out we were Odia (my father is). Well, I don't know the language, and she asked me some stuff in Odia, which was pretty embarrassing. But at least

I'm one of the few in my class who can speak Hindi fluently (since my mother is from Bhopal), and in MY class, that's a VERY rare ability. BTW, Mom keeps asking Dad to teach me Odia, but I think he's just waiting for the perfect moment to surprise us with his language-teaching skills!

This went on for a while, and for some reason, Madhusmita always sits with me on the bus, while Shiv sits behind us. The reason is that I'm more vulnerable at the back because he keeps launching *"Air raids"*—sudden ambushes of books, punches, tickles, etc.—and I hate it.

I got on the bus thinking of what I was going to face today. It was tickles. As soon as I sat down, a shower of tickles fell on me. I sank under my seat and pulled out my one-foot-long wooden scale from my bag. I got up to get the high ground and thrust my scale at Shiv like a sword.

Shiv looked dumbstruck, but after a minute, he made the biggest brain move—he took my scale. What happened next was shocking.

The boy sitting next to him snatched the ruler out of Shiv's hand and gave it back to me. The boy and Shiv fought for the rest of the ride until I reached home.

I kept wondering if they were still fighting, as I got down from the bus before Madhusmita, Shiv, and the boy.

Chapter 3:

The Elections- Posters, Votes, and Dreams

I sat in my normal place next to Vishnudas, who was talking animatedly to Rajeev, who was seated opposite him. I was waiting for Shloka Ma'am to come and start the first period – Science.

After Shloka Ma'am entered, an announcement was made in the Public Address (PA) system: "The school elections are going to start from Monday, and if you want to participate in the elections, then you can attach a file to the mail which will be sent today itself. Auditions shall end on 26th July 2022." I was thrilled, I could be Head Boy if people voted for me! "I would also like to inform that $1^{st} - 4^{th}$ class students are not permitted to be Head Boy, Head Girl, and Captains; they can only become Assistants." Okay, Assistant Head Boy is still fun.

The next day everyone was talking about winning the elections. I had made my own poster just like many others. There was a blanket of posters on the wall – it looked as though the school just got some free wallpaper – I saw that Nagesh was running for <u>*ALL*</u> the positions. I was running for two positions like the majority – Assistant Unity House Captain and Assistant Head Boy – Vishnudas, who had been boasting that he would become Head Boy, seemed to have "Forgotten" to sign up.

When Shloka Ma'am came, she really liked my poster and said it was the <u>*BEST*</u> one in the class.

When I went to stick my poster, I saw that one girl named Jaya had put up so many posters that 90% of the wall was filled

ONLY with her posters, and _ALL_ of them were handmade! I stuck my poster and sat in my place so that Ma'am could continue her class, only to be interrupted by an announcement from the PA system: "Elections shall start tomorrow, further instructions shall be sent in an email, thank you." I became anxious; tomorrow was the day that would decide whether I would become Assistant Head Boy or at least Assistant House Captain.

At around the 4th period, we headed towards the voting booth (which was basically the cafeteria, but all the chairs were just repurposed). But you know the worst thing that happened? The Unities had to come _LAST_, and if I didn't tell you by now, I am from Unity House!

After what felt like a millennia, I finally got to vote. Of course, I voted for myself, but when I went to vote for myself as the Junior Assistant Unity House Captain, I saw that there were only _TWO_ people running for that post: me and a girl named Prateeksha (who I remembered was in my guitar class). The thing that surprised me was that in the other posts there were, like, 50 or 60 people running for it, but here it was, like, 50-50. We both had an equal chance to, like, win, and the beef was on.

Because the very next day, they were going to give the results.

As the day ended and I was going towards the bus, many random people came to me and told me that they had voted for me, and that really raised my spirits, and the next day I wanted my name to be called out over the PA system.

I sat in my place eager to hear the announcement, and it came. It hit me like Steven He's EMOTIONAL DAMAGE!

I had lost both positions. Manian was celebrating because he won, Nagesh looked around the class in disbelief that he had lost positions, some girls were crying, and I was devastated, but Sanghamitra Ma'am came and said something to relieve the crying girls: "If you are in student council, you will do nothing; you will just tell people to move left and right."

All I know is that I do not want to stand in front of a crowd and tell them where to move, so I felt better.

Chapter 4:

The Poster Incident

It was around Ganesh Chaturthi, but we didn't have any long holidays at school like in Mumbai. It was just a normal school day until the 5th period.

They took us to the skating rink. Apparently, they were going to teach us how to make a Ganesha out of clay, well, it was just a free period because literally nobody was listening to what the teacher was telling us. Peter, Nagesh, and I were discussing who was the sus'iest between the three of us, well, it was pretty easy because both Peter and Nagesh were wearing red as they both were from Freedom.

"I WOULD PLEASE REQUEST THE CHILDREN TO LISTEN TO ME!" All the conversations stopped abruptly, as they saw that the teacher had already created a clay Ganesha out of the mould beside her. "And now I am going to teach you how to make Ganesha without a mould."

The silence caused by the sudden explosion of noise only lasted a few minutes, after which the students sunk back to their own world. Nagesh, Peter, and I started chit-chatting until Prateeksha came along.

"Hi, Amritash," she said. "Er- Hi?" I responded awkwardly; I couldn't understand why the heck she came like that with Preeti beside her. "Why are you here?" I finally asked. "Ohhh," she said rhythmically, "I was just asking. *Why didn't you win the elections?*"

That was it. My veins exploded; I wished I could throw her out of the school, but I didn't want to give her the pleasure of teasing me, so I simply said, "Yeah, because I guess I'm just not popular yet, since I recently joined this school." "Oh yes, I also joined last month." I didn't want to answer that because I joined the month before last, well, I didn't have to answer that as she said, "Oh, well then bye!"

Then she and Preeti went away giggling.

By then, time was up, and we went to the washroom because it was lunch break.

The posters were still pinned to the wall; some of them were gone because the elections were over, and there was no point for them to be stuck without a purpose. Hence, there was no longer a blanket of posters; the posters were just scattered around the walls unevenly.

As I went towards my classroom, I saw that someone had torn Nagesh's poster. I went to inspect it, and just at that precise moment, Arjun came.

"YOU TORE NAGESH'S POSTER!?!" he cried. "NO!" I said, "I was just checking it." But he was not listening; he ran into the class saying, "I'll tell NAGESH now only!"

Some seconds later, Nagesh came out of the classroom and said, "YOU TORE MY POSTER!?" "No, I didn't." "Oh yes, you did." "No, I didn't!" "Oh–h–h I know you did." By now I could see through that mask of Nagesh, and he was laughing. "NO I DIDN'T!" "Oh yes, you did, HEY EVERYONE, AMRITASH TORE MY POSTER!" I grabbed his jacket and yelled out, <u>*"NO I DIDN'T!"*</u>. I burst into tears, it was a false accusation, and no one was ready to listen to me. Hearing the noise, Shloka Ma'am came.

I told her what had happened, and she scolded Nagesh and Arjun, but I wanted more. This wasn't some pity anger like I had with Prateeksha. There was a <u>*WILDFIRE*</u> inside me, and I needed a TSUNAMI to cool it down.

Chapter 5:

Peacing It Out

After the poster incident, school life for me was no longer the same.

Shloka Ma'am had changed my place. Now I was sitting with a girl named Adheera. She is not the best in academics, and that is what annoys me. She is always copying from me and getting good marks just because she is sitting next to me. It all feels unfair. And whenever I tell Shloka Ma'am, she just tells her not to do it, but obviously she never obeys.

On friendship day, Telugu class became Arts class because we needed to buy "Friendship Bands" and tie them to our best friends IN class. Now, all the best friends I have in class have some other best friends. So, I had to tie the band with Adheera.

Also, after befriending Nagesh, *I THINK* my studies have decreased, but my drop was nothing compared to Nagesh's.

Nagesh had made best friends with Nakul, who also was not the best in academics. I think Ma'am just made Nagesh sit with Nakul because she needed to change Nakul's behavior, but unfortunately the complete opposite happened.

The school had just started something known as a Class Library. While they were announcing it in the assembly some random boy raised his hand and said that he had ten books. That seemed like a big number to the principal, because she looked surprised. But to me that number was a joke; I have over one HUNDRED books easily. In my school in Djibouti, we had a book reading challenge, and during each academic year, we were supposed to read at least 25 books. Because I am passionate about reading, our school principal there gave special permission to get books issued from the senior section too. Oh, I terribly miss my Djibouti days. Such lovely days in a beautiful tiny nation. Wish I could go back!

Now my school here introduced the worst thing in the universe: an _EXTRA_ period called Lang Lab, and its grim purpose is to build fluency, which I have loads of, _BUT_ it's _MANDATORY_.

I think life without me did not suit Nagesh, because he asked if we could be friends again in PE Class.

I was even devastated by the poster incident, so at first, I was hesitant but there was no other choice.

Nagesh and I were *FRIENDS* again.

Hey! Guess what? Something super interesting happened after Friendship Day! It was my 9th birthday, and you won't believe it—my Chachu (my dad's younger brother) and Dadi (my paternal grandmother) came all the way from Dubai, and my dad came from Mumbai! My mom made this HUGE chocolate cake for me to take to school, and I brought chocolates too for everyone in my class and on the bus!

But here's the thing: I couldn't invite any friends over for my birthday party because I'm new at school, and the parents of my new friends didn't really know us well. So, I thought they wouldn't send their kids to my house. I even tried asking my friends for their parents' phone numbers so my mom could call them, but you know how kids are—they didn't remember their parents' numbers!

So, since we couldn't have a kids' party at my house (which made me a bit sad), my mom had a great idea! She decided to take me to Snow World to celebrate my 9th birthday! Yay! So, Mamaa, Papaa, Dadi, Chachu, and I went to Snow World.

It was SO much fun, but OMG, it was super cold inside! We could only stay there for two hours, but I could only handle that freezing cold for half an hour! I started to shiver and felt like I was about to freeze! So, we came out pretty quickly and headed to a nearby restaurant for dinner.

What a birthday!

Chapter 6:

M.A.N.

HOORAY!!!

Almost the entire first floor exploded with noise, and I could understand.

This was the first field trip I can remember; my parents said that I had gone for a field trip in nursery to a "Hardware Store," while we were in Mumbai.

Now I Know what you are thinking "Why did your school take you to a Hardware store?" Well even I don't know why. But <u>THIS</u> time they were taking us to <u>BIRLA SCIENCE MUSEUM.</u>

Besides this news, Shloka Ma'am wasn't coming for a while so we had to seek refuge in other classes, because if I haven't told you yet, our class, when left without a teacher can do wonders, and not in a good way.

One day prior to D-Day, Shloka Ma'am was absent, <u>*AGAIN*</u>, and we had to go to Sanghamitra Ma'am's class, where we had a <u>*BLAST*</u>! Well except for the part where we played "Pass the Parcel", and whoever lost had to do a greatly embarrassing task given by Sanghamitra Ma'am. Well, when I caught the "Parcel" I had to walk like a girl, but I just stood there… embarrassed.

I also figured out that the boy who sat with us in the bus and even now, was named Shantanu Bhaskar.

We both sat together and when Nagesh sat with us while Sanghamitra Ma'am was making us play "Dumb Charades" (Girls vs Boys), he spoke like an activist.

"There is no difference between girls and boys!" "Equality" "All of us will win" Blah Blah…..Yada Yada!

Me and Shantanu did not like it, then we realized something:

We both understand each other,

We both felt the same way about Nagesh – he just wasn't our cup of tea.

WE COULD START A MOVEMENT!

And hence to celebrate this newfound animosity we gave Nagesh a nickname that I can't tell. And then we both became the founders of M.A.N. [Movement Against Nagesh].

Back then, I really liked reading about geo-political history from around the world and found all those big movements super fascinating! Wow, we could have one in school too.

Chapter 7:

Blank Books- A Day at the Museum

After Shantanu and I created M.A.N., we needed some members.

So, after we got onto the bus, we asked Shiv if he wanted to join M.A.N., and, surprisingly, he said yes!

But a movement is like a community, and we needed more people, so tomorrow's field trip was a great way to increase members.

After breakfast, we got ready, and as we were going down to the PA, Shloka Ma'am told us to take our notebooks and get onto the buses. WE WERE GOING TO BIRLA SCIENCE MUSEUM!

The trip to the science museum was about 1 hour. All of us had a rap battle (sort of), but most of the ride I just slept, so I really don't know what happened on the bus.

When we got to the science museum, we found that it was located on a cliff, and then Vishnudas had this idea that we were going to get down by parachutes! Well, sadly, we didn't get down by parachutes; we went <u>UP the road</u>.

There was nothing much, so my book remained blank, except for some doodles I did because I was bored.

Suddenly I heard some wowing, and I was eager to see what it was, and it was an <u>ENTIRE SKELETON REPLICA</u> of some long-necked herbivorous dinosaur. I saw a real dinosaur skeleton showcased in a mall in Dubai while visiting my Chachu one summer.

After that, things were much more fun. We saw some Space Launch Vehicles (SLVs) and some aeroplane models, but then we went to the best place yet…

<u>*THE EXPERIMENT ROOM!!!*</u>

Weird buttons you have to press to see bizzare rays of electricity, spin wheels to see some random boy running, and go into a room made of glass only to get hit on your face, because the exit is everywhere! The best place to be!

Then, after that, it got boring again. We had to see some unclothed statues and some old porcelain dolls.

Then, after that, we had to go home, but then I realized that I had not asked anyone to join M.A.N. But then I would have another opportunity to ask.

Chapter 8:

Expressions 2022

A month after the Birla Museum visit, we got 2 more members to join M.A.N. – Arjun and Vishnudas. This seemed ironic because Arjun was the reason Nagesh and I are enemies now, but when it comes to having more members, you just have to take anyone. That's rule No. 1, so write that down, will you?

After we got five members, Nagesh decided to make another movement to oppose M.A.N., so he created M.A.A. [Movement Against Amritash], which is pretty much a copy of M.A.N. I tried to explain to Nagesh that he has to give me a royalty fee whenever someone joins him, as his idea is copied from me, but he never listened. Well, I think copying my movement isn't illegal because I never patented or copyrighted it, but I still deserved some compensation.

Nagesh's movement wasn't as popular as mine, he only got 1 member (Nakul). I think it's because no one could have a reason to hate me, while Nagesh was sort of like the teacher's pet and a big complainer, so naturally, other kids didn't like him.

During this time, there was a buzz about something called _"Cultural Fiesta – Expressions 2022-23."_ I've seen posters about it everywhere and even students telling each other that they "signed up" for it.

I thought I could ask Shiv and Shantanu about it, but just as I went to ask them, they said that they had signed up!

But then, one particular day, Ma'am asked us to tell what we were doing for the Cultural Fiesta, and at that moment I realized that the Cultural Fiesta was something like a talent show or maybe a competition, I guess? I asked Shloka Ma'am if I could sign up for the Cultural Fiesta.

But she said that it was too late, but she did tell me I could sign up for *Kala Khoj*, some sort of prize-less competition. *Kala Khoj* in English translates to Talent Search. I only thought that signing for it would increase my popularity count. So, for now, I just hope my *Kala Khoj* goes well.

Chapter 9:

Seven Members

My *Kala Khoj* went TERRIBLE!

Believe me, I didn't even WANT to sing *"We Are the World"*; I wanted to sing *'The World's Smallest Violin,"* but my mother made me sing it. Well, she insisted that the song sung at school should be meaningful and inspirational. I had to listen to her, as she was already upset that I missed participating in the main competitions. She's quite particular about me taking part in extracurricular activities. You know how moms tend to take everything too seriously.

But the good thing is that M.A.N. has got its seventh member – Abdul.

According to the title, this is the end of the chapter, and I don't even know what to write next, so to stretch this chapter, I'm gonna round up the whole Cultural Fiesta here.

So, this is how the whole Cultural Fiesta thing went:

After the *Kala Khoj*, we had Mono Acting. I liked Manian and Preeti's. Another girl from 4B did an act on trees that was so long that it crossed the 10-minute time limit.

Then we had Coding, in which they took the participants to the Computer Lab. If you want to know what happened, you need to go and ask someone else.

For the Spelling Bee, it was the same; they took the participants to another place, with the only difference being that there were three rounds.

I've pretty much summed up the whole Cultural Fiesta thing here. But don't forget about the winners!

Preeti won first prize in Mono Acting (If you're wondering what Preeti and Manian did for their Mono Act, well, Manian played a Pizza Delivery man who was getting confused because an old Amma kept asking for weird requests like chutney on pizza. Preeti played Aryabhata and Alia Bhatt; it was a comedy act on how similar the two names are), but what surprised me was that Nagesh had bagged third prize in Mono Acting. Well, to me, his act was the cringiest of them all! He literally ate ONE spoon of noodles and then he got a _STOMACHACHE!_ (He did an act on healthy eating.)

The 5th graders had a Ted Talk, and next year I think I'm going to sign up for that.

But one thing is for sure – I'm not forgetting to sign up.

Chapter 10:

M.A.N.'s Peak Time

The last two months of term one were pretty fun, but the fun just had to end because something interesting happened: our exams started. Interesting – YES! Fun? – TOTALLY NOT!

These aren't our final exams; these are our term exams, but I think they will have an effect in the future, so for now, I really need to get good marks.

But recently, Madhusmita, Vishal Dev, and Adheera joined M.A.N. Vishal was completely random. Shloka Ma'am made me sit next to Vishal, and completely parallel to me was Nagesh. So, one day we both asked if he would join M.A.A. or M.A.N. Vishal said that he hated us both equally, but he'd rather join M.A.N., and he did.

After getting an average of 1 MILLION notes per day, our exams started. Our first exam was Technology, followed by English, Mathematics, Science, and lastly, Art.

Although the exam lasted for only about a week, it was a bit of a drag.

You might think that this was M.A.N.'s peak time because we hit double-digit membership, but you'd be wrong because after the exam, M.A.N. activities in 4C were booming!

After the exams, we always used to have a Culminating Day, but this time we were having something different: we had an SLC (Student-Led Conference).

It was just explaining stuff you learned to your parents through activities and impressing them to get good comments.

To prepare for the SLC, we were getting LOADS of free periods, and when I say loads, I MEAN "Loads." We were getting so many free periods that there was actually only ONE real period – the first period, every day.

The fact is that we weren't really USING the periods for what they were meant for – and by we, I mean the vast majority.

We had so much free time that Hardik, Priyanka, Srinidhi, and Arjun created a PIZZA STORE. They didn't sell real pizza; they just sold paper with pizzas drawn on it. They did pretty well in sales. Their company made a profit of more than –

1OOOOOOOOOOOOOOOOOOOOOOOOOOOOOOOOOOOOOOOOOOOOOOOOOOOOOOOOOOOOOOOOOOOOOOOOOOOOOOOOOOOOOOOOOOOOOOOOOOOOOOOOOOOOOOOOOOOOOOOOOOOOOOOOOOOOOOOOOOOOOOOOOOOOOOOOOOOOOOOOOOOOO DOLLARS AND 1OOOOOOOOOOOOOOOOOOOOOCENTS!

Even I bought a pizza for ten quintillion rupees. We didn't give them real money; we just gave them little chits with numbers written on them, but they were still the first centillionaires in the world.

Now, did you see what the vast majority was doing? We weren't really using our time for what it was meant for.

All I ever did for the SLC was make chits with questions written. I also increased my workload because I lost Shloka Ma'am's sketch pen, which was eventually found under her table.

You must be thinking, how was this M.A.N.'s peak time? Well, what do YOU think we were doing in the free periods? Well, the answer is, we were "teasing" Nagesh, and well, he was teasing me more!

A few days prior to the SLC, my first cousin from Mumbai, Sumatrika Didi, came home before the Bathukamma (Navratri-Dussehra) Festival.

I somehow made her join M.A.N., and for the record, she didn't even KNOW who Nagesh was!

So, kids, that's what you call MOBILIZING!

That's rule No. 2, so write that down, will you?

I had to go to the SLC WITH her. Sumatrika Didi is just seven months older than me, so we are of the same age and grade.

We didn't see Nagesh, but we met Shantanu's and Vishnudas's parents during the SLC.

I got 40/40 in Science, and I took my Mom, Dad, Sumatrika Didi, my Mami (Maternal Aunt), and my Mamu (Maternal Uncle) for a stroll. Sumatrika Didi insisted that we should go to some other classes. I was hesitant at first, but after we got permission from a teacher, we went, and boy, was I jealous! They had created entire PALACES out of LEGO! I wish we could have built LEGO palaces, but it was in fifth grade, so probably next year we'd do it, and if we don't, I don't even KNOW what I'll do!

Hurray!! With the Bathukamma-Dussehra holidays round the corner, I had to pack my bags because my mother decided that I was going to Mumbai with Sumatrika Didi. If I stayed home, she said I'd just end up watching TV all day.

You know, my dad was then working in Mumbai, and my maternal grandparents *(Nana & Nani)* moved with us to Hyderabad to help look after me. So, it was also the perfect chance to spend some time with him in Mumbai!

Chapter 11:

Mumbai: A Walk Down Memory Lane

I was traveling to Mumbai with *Sumatrika Didi*, *Mamu*, and *Mami* on a Sleeper Coach Bus, the most comfortable way to travel from Hyderabad to Mumbai.

We had to wait longer than expected for the bus at the boarding point. We even had enough time to go around the mall, and I made the horrendous mistake of wearing a jacket, thinking it would look cool!

After the bus finally came, we tried to find our seats. In the end, we had two seats. Sumatrika Didi and I took the one-seater and played Raja Rani, a game in which we act like kings and queens, and we were trying to defeat the Mughals at Karachi, pushing them toward Iran in the hopes of taking Tehran, the capital of Iran.

You know what? Sumatrika Didi is just seven months older, but she insists on being called *Didi*-meaning elder sister!. We've always been super close. For the first five years of my life, we lived in the same locality in Mumbai, and she's my first friend. We practically grew up together! From playgroup to KG-2, we were in the same school and the same class. But then, when I turned 5, I moved to Djibouti. Even now, we still take French online classes together.

Anyway, back to the bus! While playing, I opened the window curtain to look out, and all I saw was white plastic; they had COVERED our window!

I went to see if Mamu and Mami had an open window, and they did. I ran and then started to climb the ladder, but then suddenly the bus gave a great, big lurch. With the sudden movement, I looked down. Now don't get me wrong, I'm not afraid of heights, I was just scared that the bus would move more. And there I was, with my didi telling me to go up on one side and Mamu and Mami telling me to come up on the other. I found enough courage to just jump up, and then I hit my head on a pole.

After that we ate some foxnuts, saw some things out of the window, learned about a great king whose statue was built right next to a fuel station our bus was using, and saw a cello tape that seemed to want bus domination, "we" went to "sleep."

I woke up with my head getting hit on a pole AGAIN. I had woken up in the middle of dawn. I decided to go back to sleep, but shortly after making that decision, Sumatrika Didi woke up, followed by Mami and Mamu. Our stop had come, and just as we got off, it was utter mayhem. We searched for an auto, reached my Didi's house, and then my Mami became SPEED! She made breakfast and lunch for BOTH Sumatrika Didi and Mamu, then dropped them off at the bus stop, came back, made lunch and breakfast for me, all in 1 hr, 2 mins, and 3 secs, WHOA!

It turned out that the TV wasn't working, ugh, what a bummer! So, I just doodled something(s), and then the TV guy came, but he forgot his stuff and had to go back quickly. Well, for him, quick meant 3 hrs and 45 mins.

Like, even Sumatrika Didi came home from school before that TV guy. She was pretty uncomfortable, ugh, talk about first-world problems!

And when the TV did get fixed, I watched it for maybe an hour?

But then this happened: my father decided to come to my cousin's house!

See, as I told you earlier, when we moved from Mumbai to Hyderabad, it was my MOTHER who got a job, not my father, so he stayed in Mumbai doing his old job. Instead of going to our old house, he was coming to my Mamu's house, and that's super sweet!

And when my dad came, I took his phone and made a YouTube video, and it was my first YouTube video to surpass a thousand views. In fact, it got approximately 3.5 thousand views! And if you want to subscribe to my YouTube, well, I have two channels: one of them is called Leo ball (it has a picture of the world with Africa centered) and the other one is L.P. with only 8 subscribers. Well, I think Leo ball is doing a million times better than L.P., with 98 subscribers.

And if you're wondering, I'm staying at Sumatrika Didi's home for 15 days, and 15 is greater than 9, and why 9, you ask? Well, because Navratri started, and THAT, my friend, means Dandiya!

See, Sumatrika Didi has a friend on the same floor as hers, and she told my Mami about a Dandiya fest, and Mami, being a mother, took us there.

But the other time we went to a different fest, and instead of joining the main Garba group, my Mami decided to make her own. Me and Sumatrika Didi were hesitant at first, but then it was only a matter of time before so many people joined that our Garba became HALF the size of the main Garba group! Then some police killjoys came and told us to stop, as it was already 10 pm. But that wasn't the end because two people dressed as tigers came, and me and Sumatrika Didi were pretty scared, but I saw the man without the mask, and I got less scared. Heck, I got so courageous that I even pulled his tail, but Sumatrika Didi was still afraid of him.

Now only a day was left to return to Hyderabad. We went to a temple and did some pooja, but then I saw some very suspicious footprints, which turned out to be of a tyrannous, monstrous, cute little girl.

Since it was my last day in Mumbai, my Mami took me to a supermarket and let me buy anything I wanted. The first thing I bought was "Slime," and then my shoe broke, so I had to walk with one foot bare. So, the next thing I bought was shoe glue, then a pocket diary, then Oreo Red Velvet, then we went to look for shoes but failed. Then we went to my Mausa ji and Mausi's home.

BTW: My Mausa ji is the Chairperson and Managing Director of a BIG public sector company, so that's nice.

There I wrote the first entry in my diary I called *Pockuto*.

This home is pretty special to me, as it was the first place we came to after we returned from Djibouti, Africa, after our 2 years of stay there. I wish every day that I could go back to that amazing country – Djibouti. This place should be in every traveler's bucket list.

Well, my Mausa ji and Mausi's home in Chembur was also the place where I first laid my eyes on Calvin and Hobbes. At first, I didn't want to read it, but when I did, I LOVED it. I loved it so much that I even got my own Hobbes. It was a stuffed owl- the cushion, I named Henry after Harry Potter. I even created my own comic called Henry and Me. I even started my own agency just like G.R.O.S.S.; it was called L.A.R. (Life Agency of Research), and it was there that I employed my eldest sister's (my Mausi's daughter's) fiancé as a cleaner at the L.A.R. headquarters on the terrace. That was really sweet, he is awesome. BTW, I couldn't get my elder sisters, Palu Didi and Piyu Didi, to join the workforce at L.A.R., but they totally made up for it by giving me a burger treat! And OMG, it tasted super delicious!

Oh, those were good days, but for now, I was going back to Hyderabad.

Chapter 12:

Homecoming

After returning from Mumbai, it was 'back to school'. But this time, we had a Market Day where we had to shop and act like adults. I need to point out that when you say Manian, it sounds like you're saying "onion." I'll tell you a funny story about this a little later.

As Sanghamitra Ma'am was not present in 4B, her students had to come to our class.

I wanted to sit with someone I know, or still sit with Pooja (Shloka Ma'am had changed my place), but in the end, I had to sit with Namit. I regret turning down the option to sit with Sundar.

Well, I just want to say a lot of stuff about Namit but let me just explain it to you in about five words: Namit seemed a bit silly.

I mean, he didn't even KNOW how to divide, multiply, subtract, or even add! So, that meant I had to calculate HIS bill, and if anything, that's UNFAIR!

But after that, I didn't have to be with Namit, because 4C went after 4B on Market Day. The first thing I bought was the most convenient option for me – Lays Spanish Tomato Chips. Then I bought some Chiki (peanut-based sweet), oranges, chilies, Dal (pulses), and jam.

Actually, I took the jam from Kunal. I gave him a chili, and he gave me a whole jam packet, complete with a huge chunk of tic-tac!

Of course, one chili costs a lot less than a jam packet and tic-tac, but when something's free, you gotta take it, folks!

Actually, when I came to class, I thought that I had paid less. But on the day of getting our change, I got ONE RUPEE back! So that's sweet!

You know what else is sweet? My father is finally getting a job in HYDERABAD! Also, a new Spider-Man movie has been released called "No Way Home," so that's defying the rules in Marvel!

Hey, let me tell you about that funny incident! Manian bought onions, and then all the kids started teasing him, saying Manian-onion-Manian bought himself. Hahaha!

Chapter 13:

Presidential Perks and Pain

It's been 3 months and 15 days since we started M.A.N., and so far, our only opponent, M.A.A., hasn't been much of a challenge since we have 11 members to M.A.A.'s 3. The funny thing about Nagesh is that he never asks anyone to join M.A.A. It's like, how can one person have a billion opponents and the other only have three? I should have had way more competition!

Well, with M.A.N. being around for so much time, it was bound to have variants like: Vishnudas's M.A.N.O. (Movement Against No One), M.A.N.'s M.A.N. (Movement Against Nakul), Shantanu's M.A.N.N. (Movement Against Nakul and Nagesh), Arjun and Vishnudas's M.A.P. (Movement Against Priyanka), Nagesh's M.A.A. (Movement Against Amritash), and finally, the original Me and Shantanu's (Movement Against Nagesh)!

November 14th (Children's Day) was just around the corner, so I was wondering what our school was gonna do.

Plus, Shantanu invited me to his home. During the SLC, our parents exchanged their phone numbers, so his father called, and I had to go to his house.

When I reached his home, I saw that he had Pokémon cards, which I really, *REALLY* wanted, so he told me he'd give me Shaymin, although I really wanted Lucario. I guess Shaymin is better than nothing, so when I got Shaymin, Shantanu asked for it to "check for anything," and then he didn't give it to me. After having the most violent pillow fight, we decided that I'd get my own. But the next day, when we were out to search for Pokémon cards, Shantanu's father called, saying that I had forgotten my jacket, and when my father went to get the jacket, he brought Pokémon cards with him, saying that Shantanu's father had bought them for me. To be honest, that was _REALLY_ nice of him, and you know, his father's niceness didn't stop there because then he invited me to visit _RASHTRAPATI NILAYAM_ with them! If you don't know, it's the second OFFICIAL residence of the President of India. So now that President Kovind has retired, it's now President Droupadi Murmu's house. First impressions were pretty great; uh, now let me reframe that: first impressions were STUPENDOUS!

I mean, even I want a house as big as that, and I just Googled and saw that Presidential soil sold for _2000 RUPEES_, so that means our shoes are gonna cost millions! We also got our clothes wet with Presidential water and breathed Presidential air, and we went into the Presidential tunnel, which looked more like a "Backrooms" level, and then we threw Presidential rocks into a Presidential pond and saw a Presidential frog coming out of it.

And then Shantanu got a Presidential sprained ankle, so he didn't come to class the next day. We aren't in the same class, but we are on the same bus, so yeah!

Chapter 14:

Operation Spy

Well, now I know what our school is going to do on Children's Day. We are going to:

1. Watch the teachers' dance.
2. Do anything we want in the class.
3. See a magician doing "magic."
4. Eat tasty stuff.
5. Go home.

Also, M.A.N. has got the latest division; we call them Spies.

Look, Spies basically go to the interiors of M.A.A. and gather info about them, and how do they do that, you ask? Well, basically they join M.A.A. and get all of the latest secret news about M.A.A. and Nagesh! Basically, they become fake friends of his.

The first person to sign up for the Spy post was Vishnudas; then came Arjun, and then came Abdul. And by the info we were getting, we shifted our direction from Nagesh to Nakul because Nakul was cement and Nagesh was bricks, or in simple terms, Nakul was holding M.A.A. together, so if we removed Nakul, Nagesh would have only one member – Peter. Peter is the everyone-should-be-friends kinda guy, so he'll be easy to remove, and then Nagesh will have to surrender to M.A.N.!

Okay, so today was the day; we had no classes, and the teachers were about to dance FOR US, but just one problem: I had to sit at the back. But then the greatest thing ever happened to me!

Some kids at the front decided to get out of the carpet and started dancing, so many people started to follow them, and I took the opportunity and ran out of the carpet to get a better view and to start dancing. Then we saw some tricks from a magician, ate food, blah, blah, blah, yada, yada, and the rest is history!

Chapter 15:

The Fabric Drill

Children's Day was great to say the least, but as the end of the term came ever closer, so did our end-of-the-year Culmination Day, and after that the exams, and then 5th grade would start. I think I am going to 5th C because I am in 4th C, but the last time I thought of being with the same people all over again, it didn't come true, so better not to keep my hopes too high.

Let me share something interesting about our Culmination Day! Last year, when I was studying at the Mumbai campus of my school, we had a Culmination Day event, and the highlight of that day was a play based on the book Charlie and the Chocolate Factory by Roald Dahl. I was chosen to play the role of Mr. Willy Wonka! And you know what was the most challenging and interesting part? We did it on the Zoom platform! This was during the COVID lockdown phase when we had online school. We practiced for almost 2 months for that play. It was fun, and our section rocked!

"This year we won't be having a Culmination Day!" an announcement came. "Instead, we will be having a Sports Day, for which most of the school will be PE."

I couldn't say that I was happy, because, see, I'm not exactly the fastest in my class. I'm faster than Peter and Nagesh, I was almost faster than Vishnudas, but for now, we are at the same speed.

I don't know if I'm faster than Shiv because, in the first round, I was faster than Shiv, but in the second round, Shiv was faster, and in the third, we were both at the same speed!

And I forgot to mention that all of these races are not happening at school; they are being organized at Vijay Cricket Stadium, just so you know.

So, one day we were just starting school, and then suddenly, they told us to report to the basketball court immediately and bring our fabrics. In the basketball court, they taught us how to do a fabric drill, which basically meant holding a cloth fabric with someone else (a partner) and doing some ritual-like moves. But the basketball court was too small, so they took us to the tennis court, and if you don't know, I chose tennis as my sport, so I really got confused.

The first few days were OK. Some days after I bought my mother's dupatta (I had taken her dupatta for rehearsals) was going to tear up with daily practice, but after that, the fabric—or as they call it, the fabric drill—practice was a literal NIGHTMARE!

I got a cold and fever after like 50 days of the fabric drill practice, and I think it caused it, and literally 2 weeks of staying at home, missing the semifinals for the race, finishing the ENTIRE Harry Potter & The Philosopher's Stone, and even watching the first and second Harry Potter films, becoming a Potter-Head, and giving an Olympiad exam, they called me back to school so that I could kill myself by doing that stupid drill a GAZILLION times! And if you don't know, they were doing this for the Sports Day, but since I missed the semifinals, all I was doing for the Sports Day was that kiddish fabric drill. My partner – Vishnudas – was absent, so I had to perform with a boy from 4A – Anmol. And there were lots of other things besides racing and the fabric drill, like karate and gymnastics. Oh! I forgot to mention that Abdul broke his middle finger, but he still participated in the Sports Day. He had a cast around his arm, and he was allowed to be at the front of the line wherever he liked, so yeah.

My *Nana and Nani* came for Sports Day, and that was so sweet of them! They even told me that our fabric drill was the best out of all the performances on Sports Day! Take that everyone else! You know, family really knows how to cheer up a child, especially when he's feeling down about not being able to participate in the race.

And BTW, about my Olympiad exams, I got school rank 1 in one of them… some relief at last!

Chapter 16:

A Splashy Day

We had normal school for a while, where nothing special happened, except that when we were studying, the music from the 3rd grade practicing kept coming in through the window, and it really wasn't helping me focus. But the sound did serve as great background music. Whenever I found a question hard, or when Riyan got scolded, a really tense and dramatic background music started playing.

And if you don't know, we practiced our fabric drill on a song from Baahubali, and if you don't know what Baahubali is, then go watch it, it's a great film.

BTW, when Sumatrika Didi, visited us in Hyderabad, we visited Ramoji Film City and saw the set of Baahubali, and if you don't know what Ramoji Film City is, then go there, it's a great place.

It turns out that the 5th Graders were having a class party, and so the 4th Graders were jealous and annoyed the teachers so much that they, in turn, annoyed the school authorities so much that we finally had a class party! I thought that a class party would be like a real party (with food, music, dance, and fun activities), but instead, we just had to bring home cooked food and share. I had to bring samosas and cake for our whole class, which I brought from home.

So, on the day of the class party, Shiv and I sat together with two paper plates in front of us. I distributed the samosas, and at the end, I distributed the cake. But the whole class didn't want my cake, as their little tummies were already full, so I distributed my cake to the teachers. The only problem was, I couldn't walk; my stomach was so full that I could barely walk. Then I went to wash my face and hands, and all of the water fell over me.

I was wet, cold, and miserable, and I went back to class wanting to go home and just change my clothes really badly. The class party was totally not how I imagined.

I imagined it would be great to have some of the food from someone else and hear Vaibhav shouting, BIRYANI, BIRYANI! But instead, it ended miserably.

Chapter 17:

The Last Days of Grade 4

So, since we will be having half days when the exams start, for most subjects, it was pretty much the last class. So, in this chapter, I'm gonna tell you how each class's last day went.

ART: We did a drawing of a statue, which I was very good at, and we had to revise, which I didn't know how to do, so I doodled an entire page of my rough notebook.

TENNIS: We did what we usually do every class. Nagesh challenged me to a fencing duel and kept poking me with a tennis racket. In return, I raised my racket to poke him back, but oh, it accidentally hit him. Not wanting it to seem like an accident, I just said, "That's how real fencing is!"

PE: We played cricket, and I skipped Robotics.

GUITAR: We learned the C scale (Sa-re-ga-ma-pa-dha-ni-sa).

MATH: We prepared for the exam.

SCIENCE: We prepared for the exam.

ENGLISH: We prepared for the exam.

ROBOTICS: IDK, I skipped it.

HINDI: We prepared for the exam.

TELUGU: We had a slip test.

And finally...THE LAST CLASS OF FOURTH GRADE!: We could do whatever we wanted because it was the last class.

And with this, even M.A.N. and all its versions came to an end. **Nagesh and I agreed to be OKAYISH friends again!**

By the way, in Grade 5B, I've started my own startup – a publishing company named Willy Comics. Stay tuned to learn more about this fun-filled venture!

Hey, did you know I'm pretty much a pro at making comic strips? You can even find some of my cool cartoon creations on the Leostoons Instagram channel, the storytelling channel Ponderimus, and the geopolitics and world history channel Leoball5797 on YouTube.

If you are reading this chapter, you can choose to stop reading; this is the end of this book!

Hey, wait..wait a second! Let me finally reveal one important thing—why the book has *Dammaiguda* in the name! You must be wondering, right?? Well, *Dammaiguda* is a locality near my school, and guess what? Manian and a bunch of other kids come from that place.

And hey, just say the word *Dammaiguda* … isn't it such a FUN word?! I got so obsessed with it that now I use it as a prefix to ALL my replies at home! Like, whenever someone asks me anything, I'm just like, "*Dammaiguda* this" and "*Dammaiguda* that." I'm literally chanting *Dammaiguda* all the time—hahaha!

Acknowledgements

I named this portion of the book "Acknowledgments" because no one reads the section called "Acknowledgements"! So, this chapter doesn't really count, but if you're reading this, you must be super determined because I literally told you to stop reading just one page ago.

But hey, determination is a good thing, right? So, here's a little reward for your loyalty: You get a free subscription to Willy Comics for 3 months. Message me on my Instagram account, leostoons, to claim this reward. HURRAH!!!!

www.ingramcontent.com/pod-product-compliance
Lightning Source LLC
LaVergne TN
LVHW041557070526
838199LV00046B/2011